ANTHOLOGY FOR

The Musician's Guide
to Theory and Analysis

ANTHOLOGY FOR

The Musician's Guide
to Theory and Analysis

Jane Piper Clendinning

Elizabeth West Marvin

W. W. NORTON & COMPANY

NEW YORK · LONDON

Copyright © 2005 by W. W. Norton & Company, Inc.

Manufacturing by Quebecor World, Taunton
Book design by Rubina Yeh
Production manager: JoAnn Simony
Page composition: Roberta Flechner
Music typesetting: Music by Design

ISBN-13: 978-0-393-92576-0
ISBN-10:   0-393-92576-0

W. W. Norton & Company, Inc., 500 Fifth Avenue, New York, N. Y. 10110
         www.wwnorton.com
W. W. Norton & Company Ltd., Castle House, 75/76 Wells Street, London W1T 3QT

4 5 6 7 8 9 0

Contents

Anonymous

Minuet in D minor (from the *Anna Magdalena Bach Notebook*)

Johann Sebastian Bach (1685–1750)

Brandenburg Concerto No. 4 in G Major, second movement

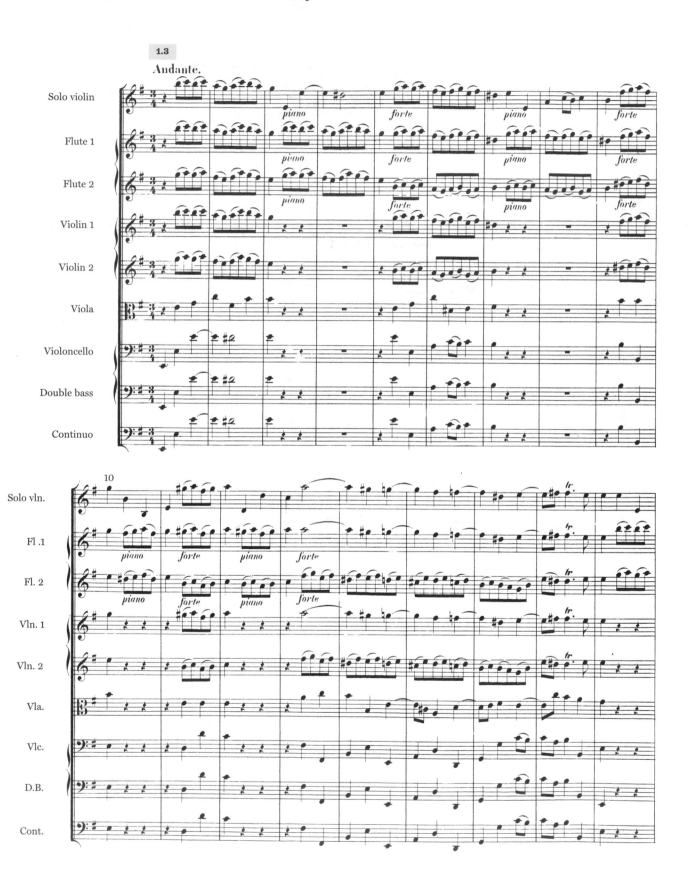

Johann Sebastian Bach
Three Chorales

"Aus meines Herzens Grunde" (No. 1)

"O Haupt voll Blut und Wunden" (No. 74)

O Haupt voll Blut und Wun - den, voll Schmerz und vol - ler Hohn,
o Haupt, zu Spott ge - bun - den mit ei - ner Dor - nen - kron,

o Haupt, sonst schön ge - zie - ret mit höch - ster Ehr und Zier, jetzt

a - ber hoch schimp - fie - ret, ge - gru - ßet seist du mir!

"Wachet auf" (No. 179)

1.9

Wa — chet auf! ruft uns die Stim —
Mit — ter — nacht heisst die — se Stun —

Wa — chet auf! ruft
Mit — ter — nacht heisst

1.10

me, Der Wäch — ter sehr hoch
de, Sie ruf — en uns mit

auf der Zin — ne: Wach
hell — em Mun — de: Wo

auf, du Stadt Je — ru — sa — lem!
seid ihr klu — gen Jung — frau — en?

Wohl - auf, der Bräut' - gam kommt,

Steht auf, die Lamp - en nehmt!

Hal - le - lu - jah! Macht

euch be - reit zu der Hoch - zeit, Ihr

müss - et ihm ent - ge - gen geh'n.

TEXTS AND TRANSLATIONS

"Aus meines Herzens Grunde" (No. 1)

Aus meines Herzens Grunde
sag' ich dir Lob und Dank,
in dieser Morgenstunde
darzu mein Lebelang,
o Gott in deinem Thron,
dir zu Lob, Preis und Ehren,
durch Christum, unsern Herren,
dein' eingebornen Sohn.

"From My Inmost Heart"

From my inmost heart
I sing to you praise and thanksgiving,
in this morning hour,
and my whole life long,
O God, upon your throne,
to you praise, glory and honor,
through Christ, our Father,
your only Son.

TRANSLATION BY CATHERINE WINKWORTH,
ADAPTED BY ELIZABETH MARVIN

"O Haupt voll Blut und Wunden" (No. 74)

O Haupt voll Blut und Wunden,
voll Schmerz und voller Hohn,
o Haupt, zu Spott gebunden
mit einer Dornenkron,
o Haupt sonst schön gezieret
mit höchster Ehr un Zier,
jetzt aber hoch schimpfieret,
gegrüsset seist du mir!

"O Head, Full of Blood and Wounds"

O head, full of blood and wounds,
full of sorrow and object of scorn,
O head, wreathed for mockery
with a crown of thorns,
O head, once beautifully adorned
with highest honor and renown,
but now highly abused:
let me hail you!

"Wachet auf" (No. 179)

Wachet auf! ruft uns die Stimme.
Der Wächter sehr hoch auf der Zinne:
Wach auf, du Stadt Jerusalem!
Mitternacht heisst diese Stunde,
sie rufen uns mit hellem Munde:
Wo seid ihr, klugen Jungfrauen?
Wohlauf, der Bräut'gam kommt.
Steht auf, die Lampen nehmt!
Hallelujah!
Macht euch bereit
zu der Hochzeit.
Ihr müsset ihm entgegen geh'n.

"Wake, Awake"

Wake up! the voice calls to us.
The guard on the high walls cries to us,
wake up, city of Jerusalem!
Midnight is the hour
they call us with clear mouths,
where are you, clever young women?
Wake up, the bridegroom comes.
Stand up, take up your lamps!
Hallelujah!
Make yourselves ready
for the wedding.
You must go out and meet him.

TRANSLATIONS BY PAUL FARSETH,
ADAPTED BY ELIZABETH MARVIN

Johann Sebastian Bach

Invention in D minor

Johann Sebastian Bach Invention in D minor

Johann Sebastian Bach

Prelude in C Major, from *The Well-Tempered Clavier,*
Book I

Johann Sebastian Bach Prelude in C Major, from *The Well-Tempered Clavier*, Book I

Johann Sebastian Bach

Chaconne, from Violin Partita No. 2 in D minor

Johann Sebastian Bach Chaconne, from Violin Partita No. 2 in D minor

arpeggio

Johann Sebastian Bach Chaconne, from Violin Partita No. 2 in D minor

Béla Bartók (1881–1945)

Bagatelle, Op. 6, No. 2

Béla Bartók

"Bulgarian Rhythm," from *Mikrokosmos* (No. 115)

Béla Bartók

"Song of the Harvest," for two violins

Ludwig van Beethoven (1770–1827)

Piano Sonata in C minor, Op. 13 (*Pathétique*),
second and third movements

Adagio cantabile.

Ludwig van Beethoven
Piano Sonata in C Major, Op. 53 (*Waldstein*),
first movement

Ludwig van Beethoven

Sonatina in F Major, Opus Posthumous, second movement

Johannes Brahms (1833–1897)
"Die Mainacht"

TEXT AND TRANSLATION

"Die Mainacht"

Wann der silberne Mond durch die Gesträuche blinkt,
Und sein schlummerndes Licht über den Rasen streut,
Und die Nachtigall flötet,
Wandl' ich traurig von Busch zu Busch.

Überhüllet von Laub girret ein Taubenpaar
Sein Entzücken mir vor; aber ich wende mich,
Suche dunklere Schatten,
Und die einsame Träne rinnt.

Wann, o lächelndes Bild, welches wie Morgenrot
Durch sie Seele mir strahlt, find ich auf Erden dich?
Und die einsame Träne
Bebt mir heisser die Wang herab!

LUDWIG CHRISTOPH HEINRICH HÖLTY

"The May Night"

When the silvery moon beams through the shrubs,
and its slumbering light scatters over the lawn,
and the nightingale flutes,
I wander sadly from bush to bush.

Shrouded by foliage, a pair of doves
coo their delight to me; but I turn away
seeking darker shadows,
and a lonely tear flows.

When, O smiling image, which like rosy dawn
through my soul shines, shall I find you on earth?
And the lonely tear
trembles, burning, down my cheek.

TRANSLATION BY LEONARD LEHRMAN,
ADAPTED BY ELIZABETH MARVIN

John Barnes Chance (1932–1972)

Variations on a Korean Folk Song, measures 1–52, 199–end

Short score (C score)

Jeremiah Clarke (1674–1707)

Trumpet Voluntary (Prince of Denmark's March)

Arranged by Sue Mitchell Wallace
and John H. Head

Muzio Clementi (1752–1832)

Sonatina in C Major, Op. 36, No. 1, first movement

Archangelo Corelli (1653–1713)
Allemanda, from Trio Sonata in A minor, Op. 4, No. 5

Archangelo Corelli Allemanda, from Trio Sonata in A minor, Op. 4, No. 5

John Corigliano (b. 1938)

"Come now, my darling," from *The Ghosts of Versailles*

Libretto by William M. Hoffman

John Corigliano "Come now, my darling," from *The Ghosts of Versailles*

1.84

Luigi Dallapiccola (1904–1975)

"Die Sonne kommt," from *Goethe-lieder,*
for voice and clarinets

*The part for piccolo clarinet is written at sounding pitch.

TEXT AND TRANSLATION

"Die Sonne kommt!" from *Goethe-lieder*

Die Sonne kommt! Ein Prachter scheinen!
Der Sichelmond umklammert sie.
Wer konnte solch ein Paar vereinen?
Dies Rätsel, wie erklärt sich's? wie?

JOHANN WOLFGANG VON GOETHE

"The Sun Comes Up!" from *Songs of Goethe*

The sun comes up! A glorious sight!
The crescent moon embraces her.
Who could unite such a pair?
This riddle, how to solve it? How?

TRANSLATION BY ELIZABETH MARVIN

George Gershwin (1898–1937)
"I Got Rhythm"

Lyrics by Ira Gershwin

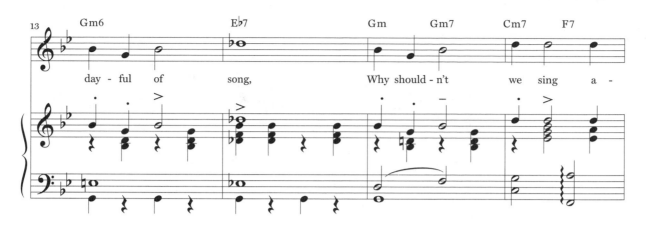

day - ful of song, Why should - n't we sing a -

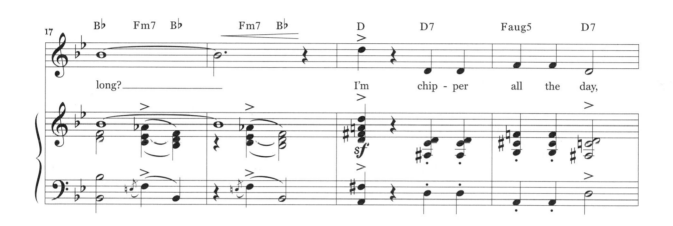

long?_____ I'm chip - per all the day,

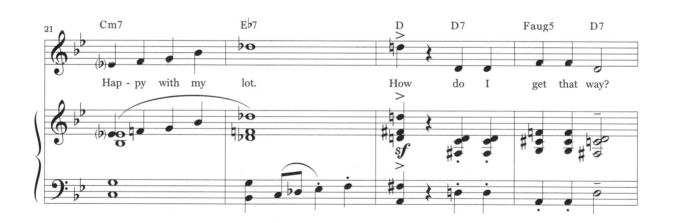

Hap - py with my lot. How do I get that way?

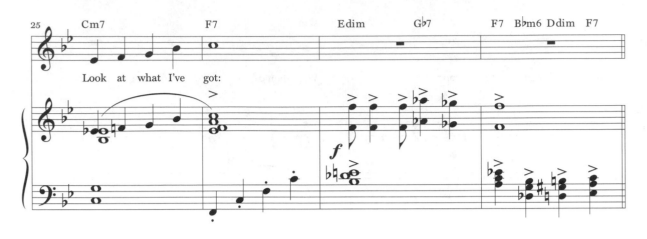

Look at what I've got:

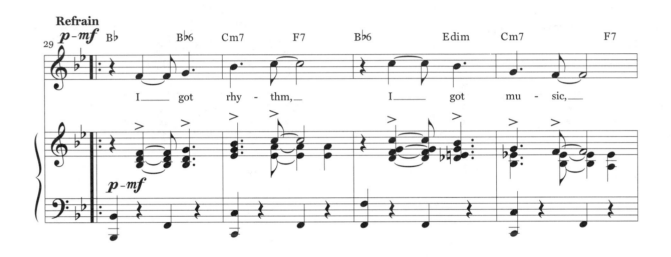

I___ got rhy - thm,__ I___ got mu - sic,__

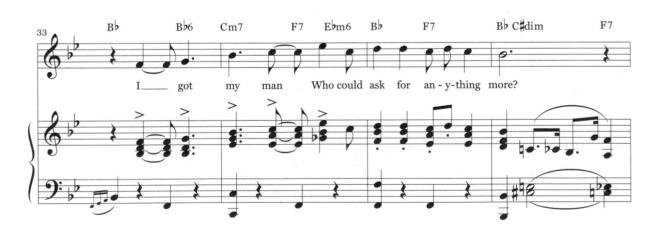

I___ got my man Who could ask for an - y-thing more?

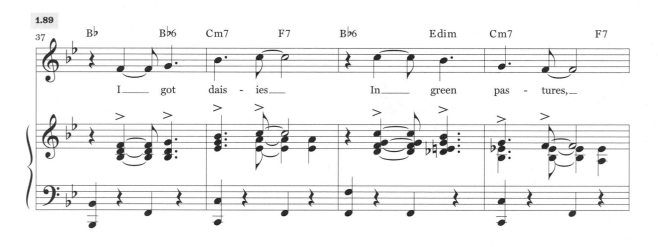

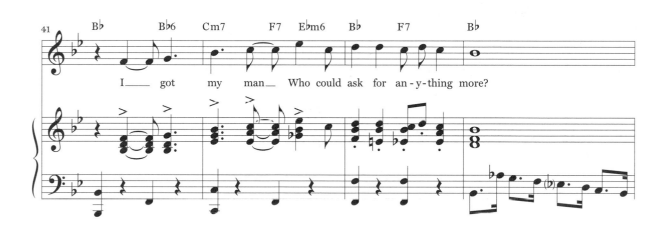

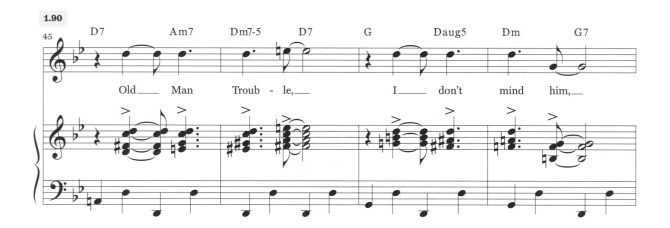

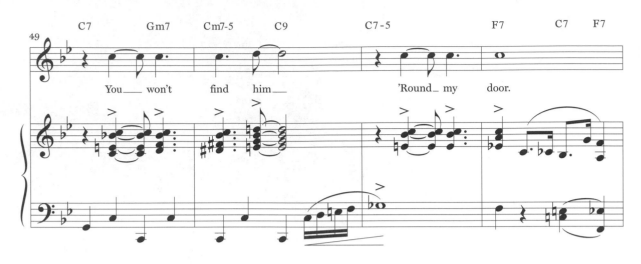

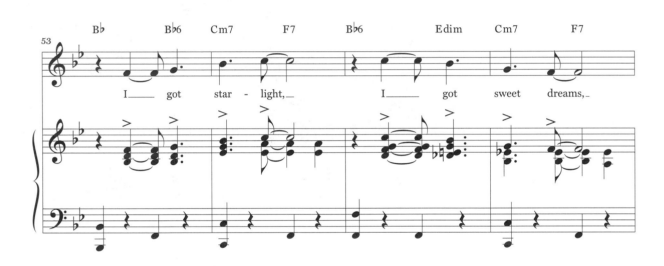

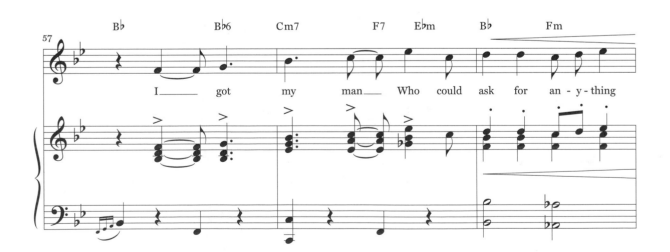

more,   Who could ask for an-y-thing more?   more?

George Gershwin
"'S Wonderful!"

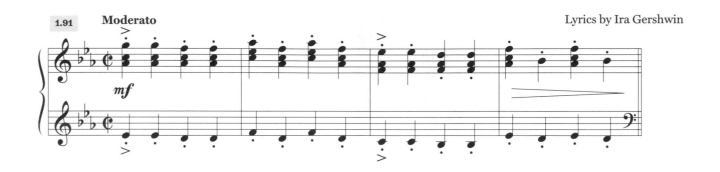

Lyrics by Ira Gershwin

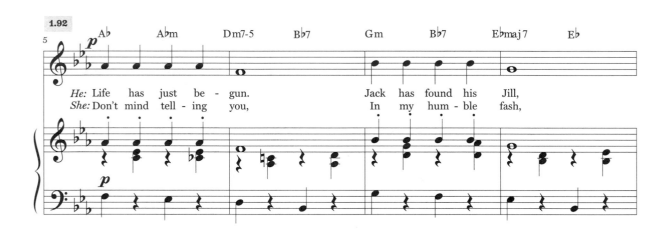

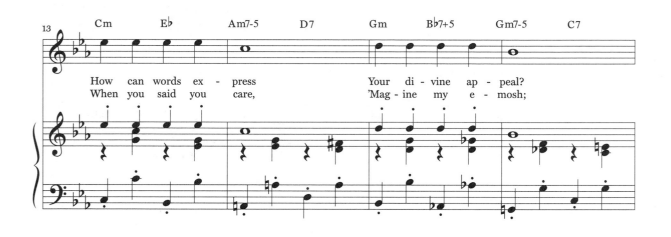

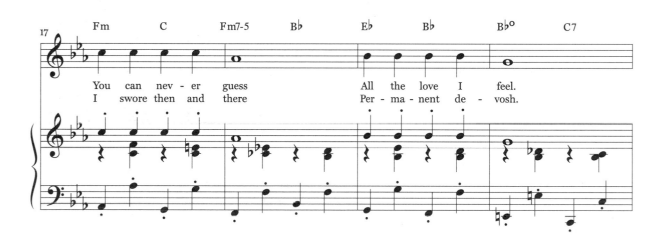

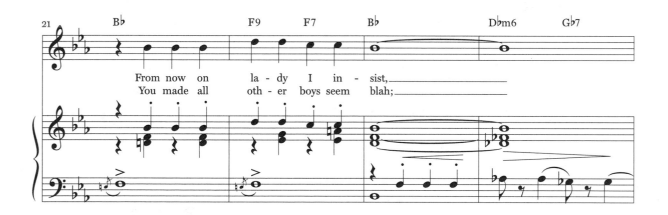

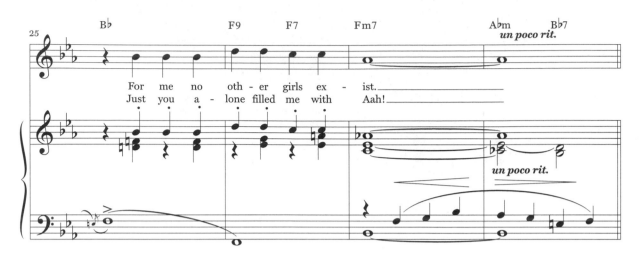

For me no oth - er girls ex - ist._____
Just you a - lone filled me with Aah!_____

1.93

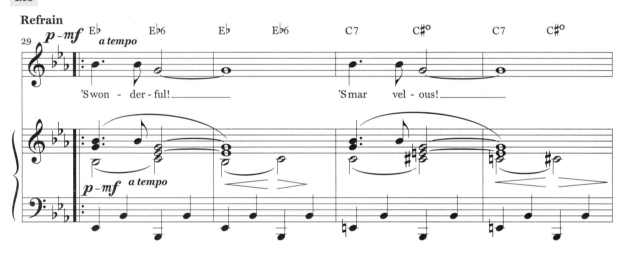

Refrain

'S won - der - ful!_____ 'S mar vel - ous!_____

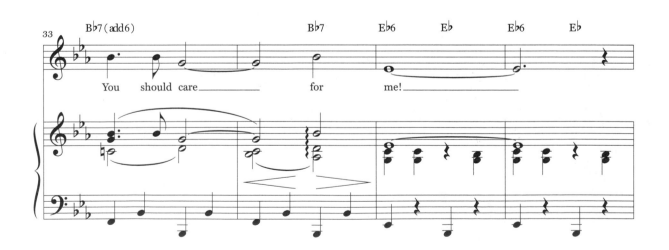

You should care_____ for me!_____

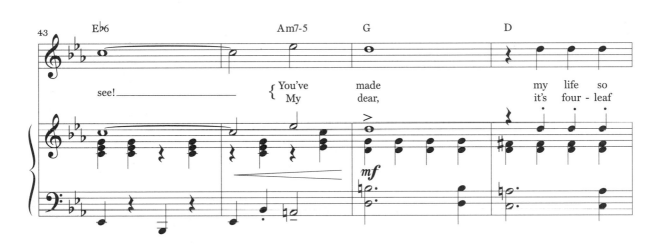

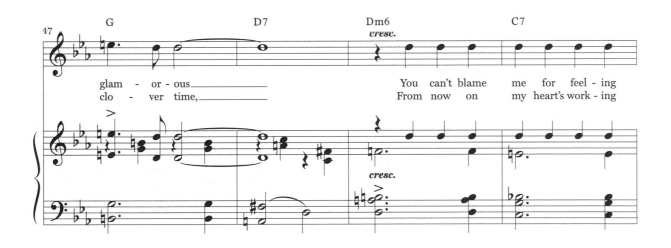

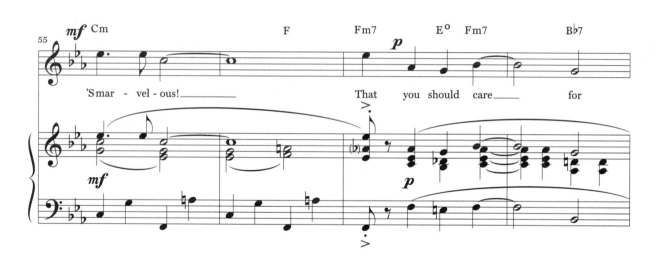

"Greensleeves"

Arranged by John Duarte

Arranged by Norbert Kraft

George Frideric Handel (1685–1759)

Chaconne in G Major, from *Trois Leçons (Three Lessons)*

George Frideric Handel

"Rejoice greatly," from *Messiah*

O daugh-ter of Je - ru - sa-lem! Be-hold,   thy king   com-eth un - to

thee,   be-hold, thy   king com - eth un - to thee.

Franz Joseph Haydn (1732–1809)

Piano Sonata No. 9 in F Major, third movement

Fanny Mendelssohn Hensel (1805–1847)

"Nachtwanderer"

Und hin und her im Tal

er- wacht die Nach - ti -

gall,

dann wie - der al - les grau,

al - les

grau _____ und stil - le.

O

wun - der-ba - rer Nacht- ge - sang, _____

von fern im Land der Strö - me Gang,

TEXT AND TRANSLATION

"Nachtwanderer"

Ich wandre durch die stille Nacht,
da schleicht der Mond so heimlich sacht
oft aus der dunkeln Wolkenhülle.
Und hin und her im Tal,
erwacht die Nachtigall,
dann wieder alles grau und stille.

O wunderbarer Nachtgesang,
von fern im Land der Ströme Gang,
leis' Schauern in den dunkeln Bäumen,
irrst die Gedanken mir,
mein wirres Singen hier
ist wie ein Rufen nur aus Träumen,
mein Singen ist ein Rufen,
ein Rufen nur aus Träumen.

JOSEPH FREIHERR VON EICHENDORFF

"Night Wanderer"

I wander through the quiet night;
the moon floats so secretly and gently,
often out from a dark cover of clouds.
And here and there in the valley
awakens a nightingale,
then again all is gray and still.

O wonderful nightsong,
from distant places the rushing of a stream
and the soft shuddering in the dark trees
confuse my thoughts.
My clamorous singing here
is like a cry only from my dreams.
My singing is a cry,
a cry only from my dreams.

TRANSLATION BY EMILY EZUST,
ADAPTED BY ELIZABETH MARVIN

Fanny Mendelssohn Hensel
"Neue Liebe, neues Leben"

TEXT AND TRANSLATION

"Neue Liebe, neues Leben"   "New Love, New Life"

Herz, mein Herz, was soll das geben?   Heart, my heart, what does this mean?
Was bedränget dich so sehr?   What is besieging you so?
Welch' ein fremdes, neues Leben!   What a strange new life!
Ich erkenne dich nicht mehr.   I do not know you any longer.
Weg ist alles, was du liebtest,   Gone is all that you loved,
Weg, worum du dich betrübtest,   gone is what troubled you,
Weg dein Fleiss und deine Ruh',   gone is your industry and your peace,
Ach, wie kamst du nur dazu!   alas! how did you come to this?

Fesselt dich die Jugendblüte,   Are you shackled by youthful bloom,
Diese liebliche Gestalt,   this lovely figure,
Dieser Blick voll Treu' und Güte,   this gaze full of fidelity and goodness
Mit unendlicher Gewalt?   with endless power?
Will ich rasch mich ihr entziehen,   If I rush to escape her,
Mich ermannen, ihr entfliehen,   to take heart and flee her,
Führet mich im Augenblick,   in a moment,
Ach, mein Weg zu ihr zurück.   ah, my way leads back to her.

Und an diesem Zauberfädchen,   And with this magic thread
Das sich nicht zerreissen lässt,   that cannot be ripped,
Hält das liebe, lose Mädchen   the dear, mischievous maiden
Mich so wider Willen fest;   holds me fast against my will;
Muss in ihrem Zauberkreise   I must, in her magic circle,
Leben nun auf ihre Weise.   live now in her way.
Die Verändrung, ach, wie gross!   The change, alas—how great!
Liebe! Liebe! lass mich los!   Love, love, let me free!

JOHANN WOLFGANG VON GOETHE   TRANSLATION BY EMILY EZUST,
                                             ADAPTED BY ELIZABETH MARVIN

Scott Joplin (1868–1917)

"Pine Apple Rag"

Scott Joplin
"Solace"

Wolfgang Amadeus Mozart (1756–1791)

Piano Sonata in G Major, K. 283, first movement

Wolfgang Amadeus Mozart Piano Sonata in G Major, K. 283, first movement

Wolfgang Amadeus Mozart

Piano Sonata in D Major, K. 284, third movement

Wolfgang Amadeus Mozart

Piano Sonata in C Major, K. 545

Wolfgang Amadeus Mozart Piano Sonata in C Major, K. 545, second movement

RONDO.

Allegretto.

Wolfgang Amadeus Mozart
String Quartet in D minor, K. 421, third movement

Menuetto D.C.

Wolfgang Amadeus Mozart

"Voi, che sapete," from *The Marriage of Figaro*

2.85

Non so chi il tie - ne, non so cos' è. So - spi-ro e ge - mo sen - za vo - ler, Pal - pi-to e tre - mo sen - za sa - per. Non tro-vo pa - ce not - te, nè dì, Ma pur mi pia - ce lan - guir co - sì. Voi, che sa - pe - te

TEXT AND TRANSLATION

Voi, che sapete che cosa è amor,
Donne, vedete s'io l'ho nel cor!
Quello ch'io provo, vi ridirò,
È per me nuovo; capir nol so,
Sento un affetto pien di desir,
Ch'ora è diletto, ch'ora è martir.
Gelo, e poi sento l'alma avvampar,
E in un momento torno a gelar.
Ricerco un bene fuori di me,
Non so chi il tiene, non so cos'è.
Sospiro e gemo senza voler,
Palpito e tremo senza saper,
Non trovo pace notte nè di,
Ma pur mi piace languir così!

You who know what love is,
ladies, see if I have it in my heart.
I'll tell you what I'm feeling,
it's new for me, and I understand nothing.
I have a feeling, full of desire,
which is by turns delightful and miserable.
I freeze and then feel my soul go up in flames,
then in a moment I turn to ice.
I'm searching for affection outside of myself,
I don't know how to hold it, nor even what it is!
I sigh and lament without wanting to,
I twitter and tremble without knowing why,
I find peace neither night nor day,
but still I rather enjoy languishing this way.

LIBRETTO BY LORENZO DA PONTE

TRANSLATION BY NAOMI GURT LIND

Wolfgang Amadeus Mozart

Variations on "Ah, vous dirai-je, Maman"

"My Country, 'Tis of Thee" ("America")

Krzysztof Penderecki (b. 1933)
Threnody for the Victims of Hiroshima,
to rehearsal 25

ABBREVIATIONS AND SYMBOLS

Sharpen a quarter-tone.	⥮
Sharpen three quarter-tones.	⥯
Flatten a quarter-tone.	♭
Flatten three quarter-tones.	⅃
Highest note of the instrument (no definite pitch).	▲
Play between bridge and tailpiece.	↑
Arpeggio on 4 strings behind the bridge.	⦚⧚
Play on the tailpiece (arco) by bowing the tailpiece at an angle of 90° to its longer axis.	┴
Molto vibrato.	〜〜〜
Very slow vibrato with a ¼ tone frequency difference produced by sliding the finger.	∿∿
Very rapid non-rhythmisized tremolo.	⚡

ordinario	ord.
sul ponticello	s. p.
sul tasto	s. t.
col legno	c. l.
legno battuto	l. batt.

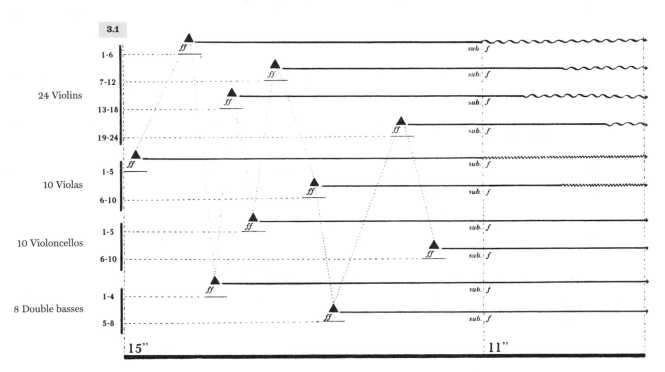

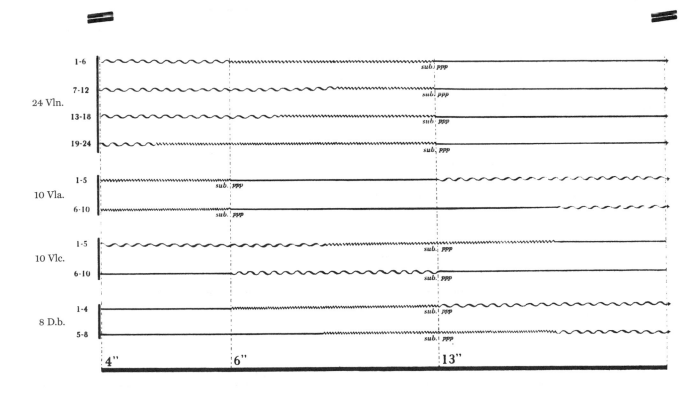

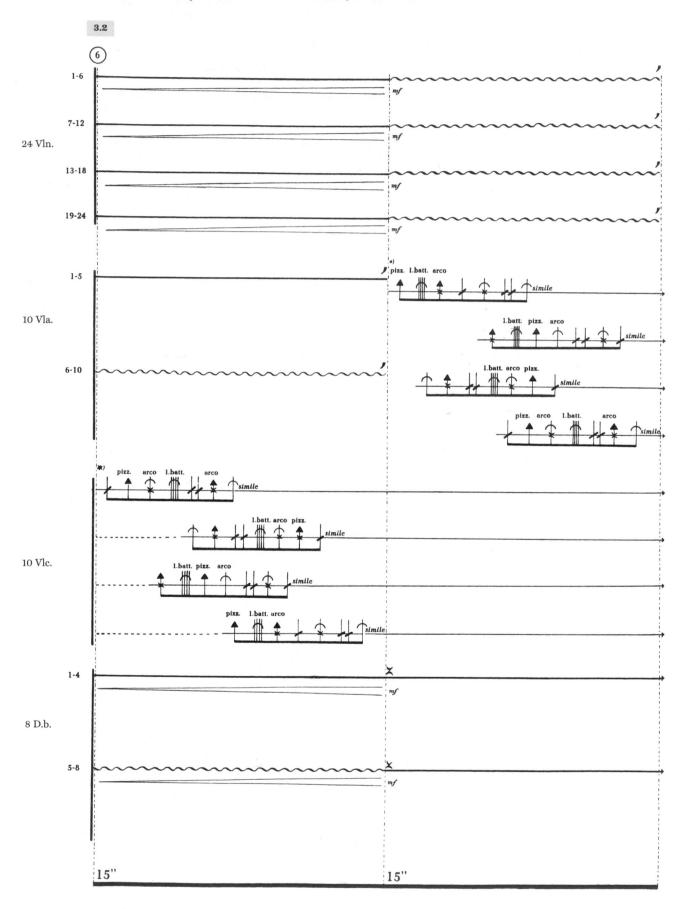

*Each instrumentalist chooses one of the four given groups and executes it (within a fixed space of time) as rapidly as possible.

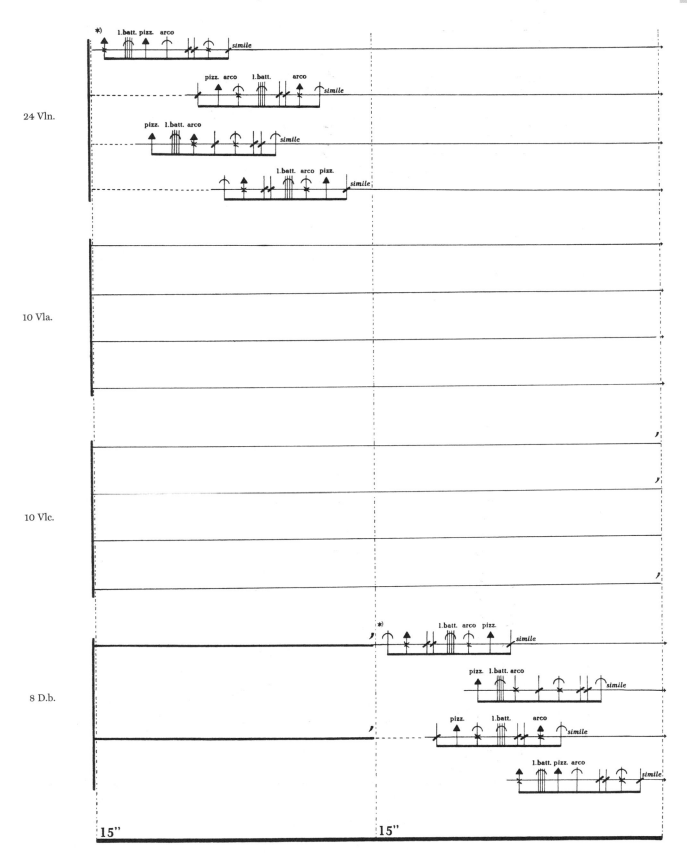

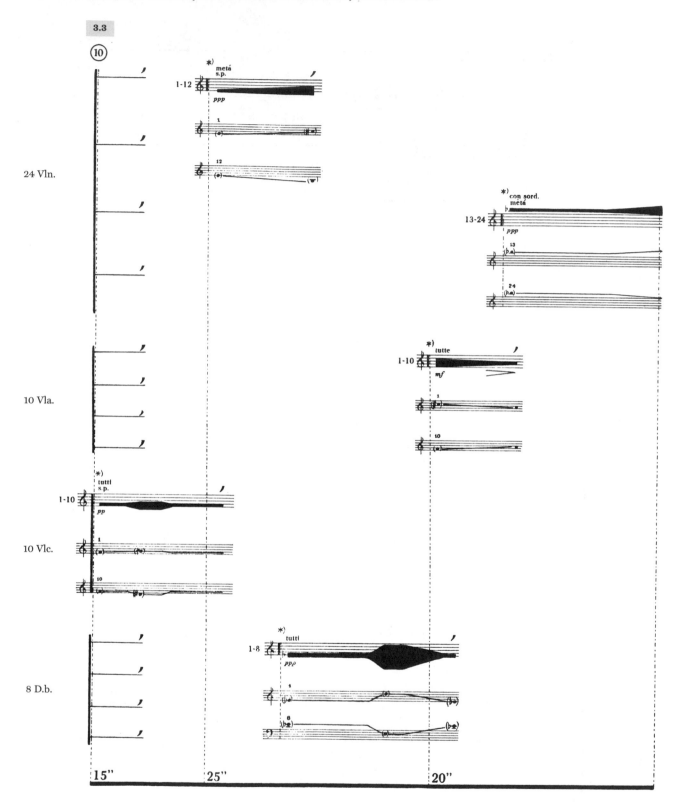

*Exact notation is given in the parts.

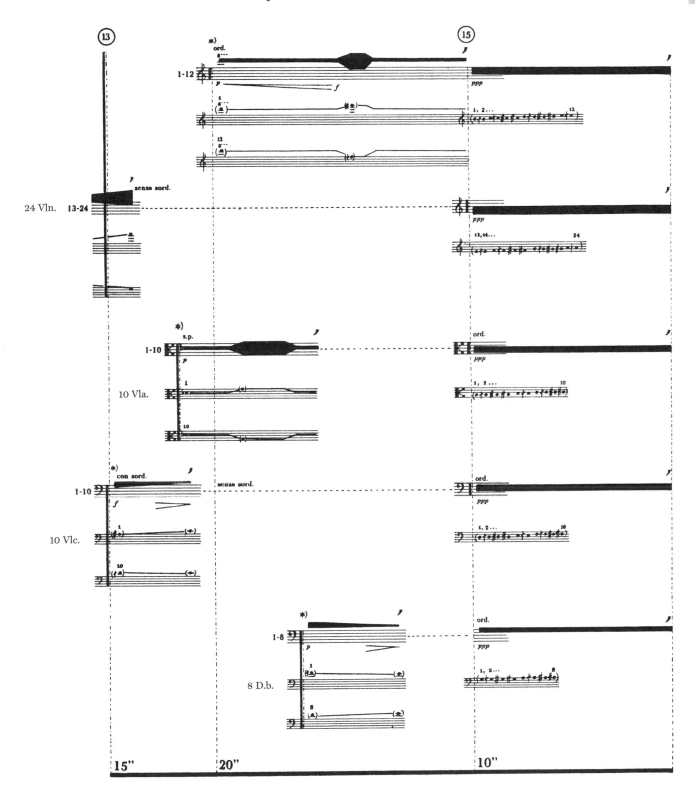

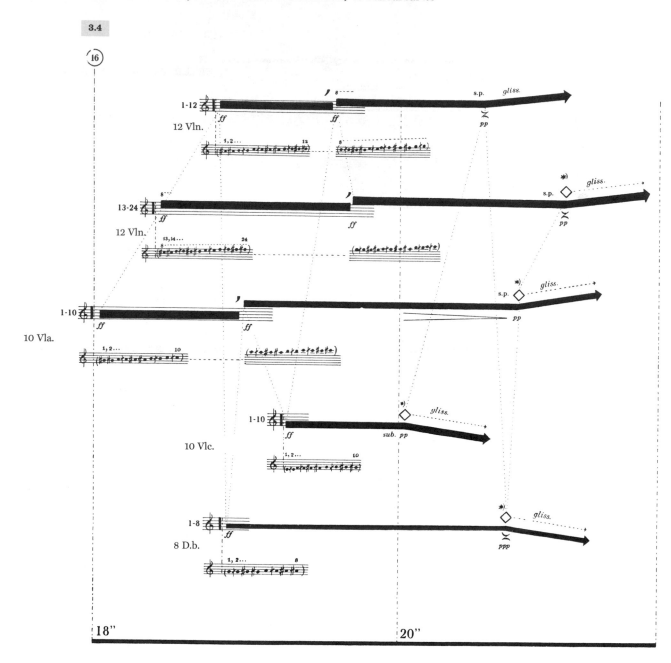

*Flageolet tones.

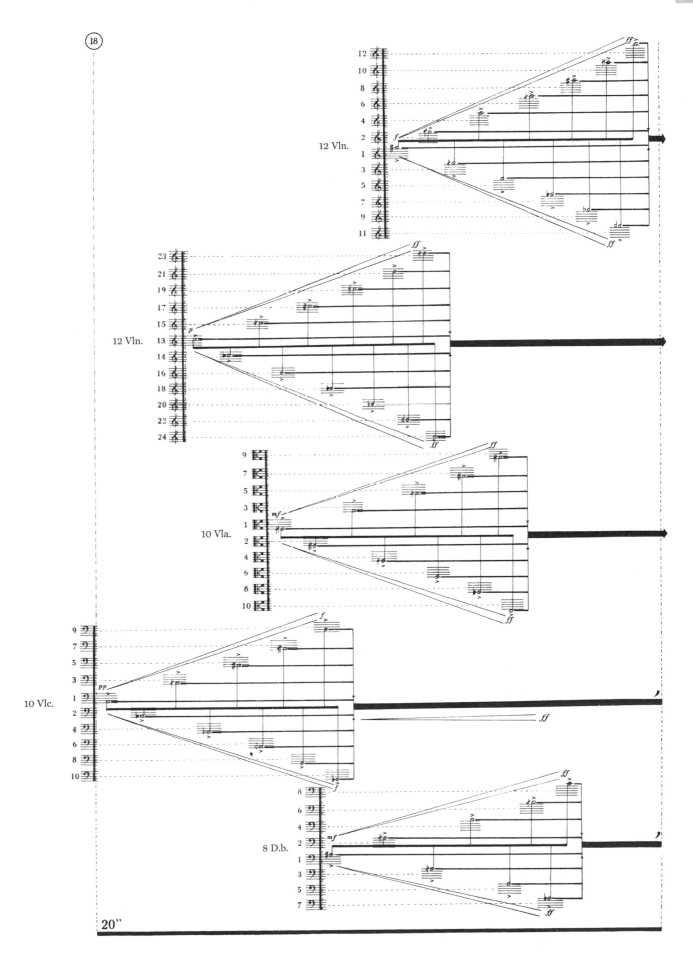

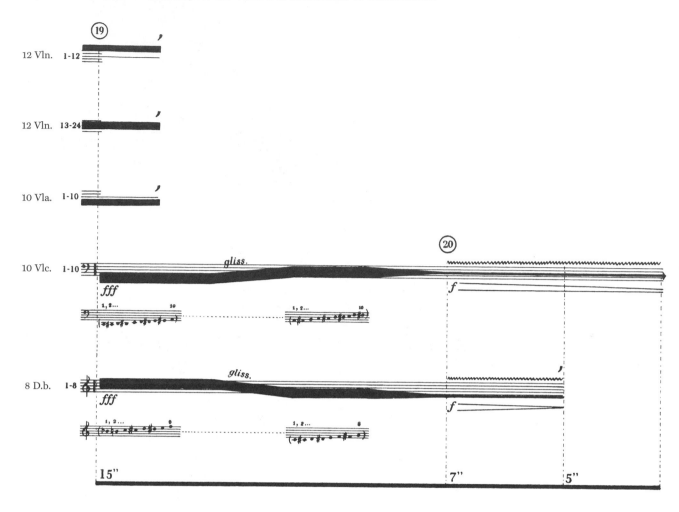

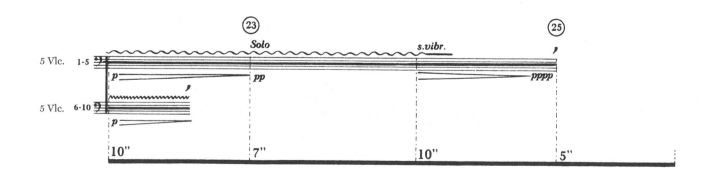

Henry Purcell (1659–1695)

"Music for a While"

Arranged by Michael Tippett
and Walter Bergmann

Steve Reich (b. 1936)

Piano Phase, patterns 1–32

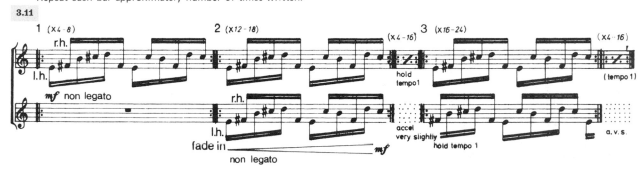

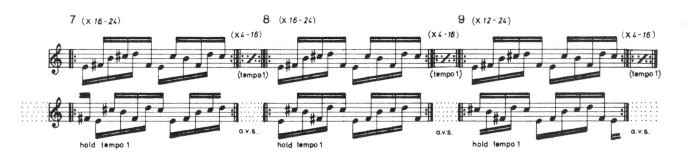

*The piece may be played an octave lower than written, when played on marimbas.

a.v.s. = accelerando very slightly.

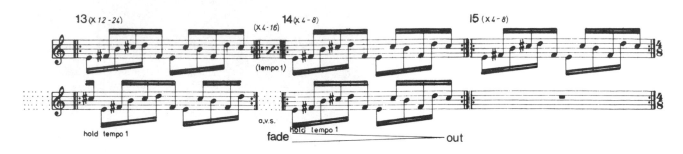

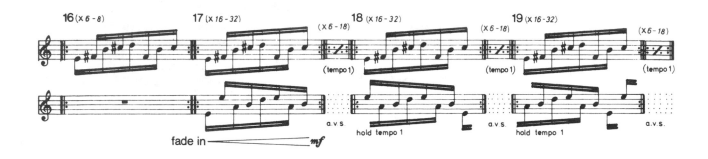

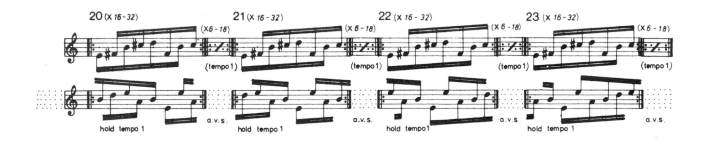

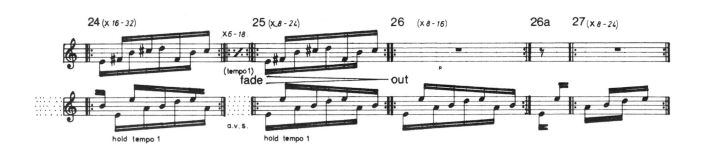

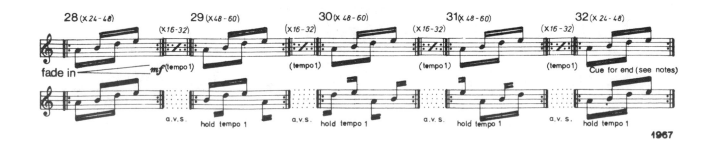

1967

Arnold Schoenberg (1874–1951)

Klavierstück (*Piano Piece*), Op. 33a

Franz Schubert (1797–1828)

"Der Lindenbaum," from *Winterreise*

TEXT AND TRANSLATION

"Der Lindenbaum," from *Winterreise*

Am Brunnen vor dem Tore
Da steht ein Lindenbaum;
Ich träumt' in seinem Schatten
So manchen süssen Traum.

Ich schnitt in seine Rinde
So manches liebe Wort;
Es zog in Freud' und Leide
Zu ihm mich immer fort.

Ich musst' auch heute wandern
Vorbei in tiefer Nacht,
Da hab' ich noch im Dunkel
Die Augen zugemacht.

Und seine Zweige rauschten,
Als riefen sie mir zu;
Komm her zu mir, Geselle,
Hier find'st du deine Ruh'!

Die kalten Winde bliesen
Mir grad' ins Angesicht;
Der Hut flog mir vom Kopfe,
Ich wendete mich nicht.

Nun bin ich manche Stunde
Entfernt von jenem Ort,
Und immer hör' ich's rauschen:
Du fändest Ruhe dort!

WILHELM MÜLLER

"The Linden Tree," from *Winter Journey*

By the fountain in front of the gate,
there stands a linden tree;
I have dreamt in its shadows
so many sweet dreams.

I carved on its bark
so many loving words;
it drew me, in joy and sorrow,
to it continually.

I had to pass it again today
in the dead of night.
And even in the darkness
I had to close my eyes.

And its branches rustled
as if calling to me:
"Come here, to me, friend,
here you will find your peace!"

The frigid wind blew
straight in my face,
my hat flew from my head,
I did not turn back.

Now I am many hours
away from that spot,
and still I hear the rustling:
there you would have found peace!

TRANSLATION BY ARTHUR RISHI,
ADAPTED BY ELIZABETH MARVIN

Franz Schubert
"Du bist die Ruh"

TEXT AND TRANSLATION

"Du bist die Ruh"

Du bist die Ruh,
Der Friede mild,
Die Sehnsucht du,
Und was sie stillt.

Ich weihe dir
Voll Lust und Schmerz
Zur Wohnung hier
Mein Aug' und Herz.

Kehr' ein bei mir
Und schliesse du
Still hinter dir
Die Pforten zu.

Treib' andern Schmerz
Aus dieser Brust!
Voll sei dies Herz
Von deiner Lust.

Dies Augenzelt,
Von deinem Glanz
Allein erhellt,
O füll' es ganz!

FRIEDRICH RÜCKERT

"You Are Rest"

You are rest,
the mild peace,
you are longing
and what stills it.

I consecrate to you
full of pleasure and pain
as a dwelling here
my eyes and heart.

Come live with me,
and close
quietly behind you
the gates.

Drive other pain
out of this breast.
May my heart be full
with your pleasure.

The tabernacle of my eyes
by your radiance
alone is illumined.
Oh fill it completely!

TRANSLATION BY LYNN THOMPSON (ADAPTED)

Franz Schubert
"Erlkönig"

3.26

TEXT AND TRANSLATION

"Erlkönig"	"The Erl King"
Wer reitet so spät durch Nacht und Wind?	Who's riding so late through night and wind?
Es ist der Vater mit seinem Kind;	It is the father with his child;
Er hat den Knaben wohl in dem Arm,	he has the boy secure in his arm,
Er fasst ihn sicher, er hält ihn warm.	he holds him tight, he keeps him warm.
"Mein Sohn, was birgst du so bang dein Gesicht?"	"My son, why do you hide, so fearfully, your face?"
"Siehst, Vater, du den Erlkönig nicht?	"See you not, father, the Erl King near?
Den Erlenkönig mit Kron' und Schweif?"	The Erl King with his crown and train?"
"Mein Sohn, es ist ein Nebelstreif."	"My son, it is a foggy patch."
"Du liebes Kind, komm, geh mit mir!	"You lovely child, come, go with me!
Gar schöne Spiele spiel' ich mit dir;	What wonderful games I'll play with thee;
Manch bunte Blumen sind an dem Strand,	flowers, most colorful, are on the shore.
Meine Mutter hat manch' gülden Gewand."	My mother has golden clothing for you."
"Mein Vater, mein Vater, und hörest du nicht,	"My father, my father, do you not hear
Was Erlenkönig mir leise verspricht?"	what Erl King is softly promising?"
"Sei ruhig, bleibe ruhig, mein Kind:	"Be calm, stay calm, my child;
In dürren Blättern säuselt der Wind."	in the dried leaves the wind is rustling."
"Willst, feiner Knabe, du mit mir gehn?	"Will you, fine lad, go with me?
Meine Töchter sollen dich warten schön;	My daughters will wait on you;
Meine Töchter führen den nächtlichen Reihn	my daughters will conduct their nightly cleansing
Und wiegen und tanzen und singen dich ein."	and swing and dance and sing to you."
"Mein Vater, mein Vater, und siehst du nicht dort	"My father, my father, can you not see
Erlkönigs Töchter am düstern Ort?"	Erl King's daughters, there in that melancholy spot?"
"Mein Sohn, mein Sohn, ich seh' es genau:	"My son, my son, I see it clear;
Es scheinen die alten Weiden so grau."	the ancient willows appear so gray."
"Ich liebe dich, mich reizt deine schöne Gestalt;	"I love you, I'm aroused by your beautiful form;
Und bist du nicht willig, so brauch' ich Gewalt."	and if you're not willing, I'll take you by force."
"Mein Vater, mein Vater, jetzt fasst er mich an!	"My father, my father, how he clutches at me!
Erlkönig hat mir ein Leids getan!"	Erl King has done me harm!"
Dem Vater grauset's, er reitet geschwind,	The father shudders, he rides swiftly;
Er hält in Armen das ächzende Kind,	he holds in his arms the groaning child;
Erreicht den Hof mit Mühe und Not:	he arrives in the courtyard, with effort and distress;
In seinem Armen das Kind war todt.	in his arms, the child was dead.
JOHANN WOLFGANG VON GOETHE	TRANSLATION BY WALTER MEYER, ADAPTED BY ELIZABETH MARVIN

Clara Schumann (1819–1896)

"Liebst du um Schönheit"

o nicht mich lie - be! Lie- be den Früh-ling, der

jung ist je - des Jahr! Liebst du um Schät - ze,

o nicht ____ mich lie - be! Lie - be die

Meer - - frau, sie hat viel Per - len klar.

TEXT AND TRANSLATION

"Liebst du um Schönheit"

Liebst du um Schönheit, o nicht mich liebe!
Liebe die Sonne, sie trägt ein goldnes Haar!

Liebst du um Jugend, o nicht mich liebe!
Liebe den Frühling, der jung ist jedes Jahr!

Liebst du um Schätze, o nicht mich liebe!
Liebe die Meerfrau, sie hat viel Perlen klar!

Liebst du um Liebe, o ja—mich liebe!
Liebe mich immer, dich lieb ich immerdar!

FRIEDRICH RÜCKERT

"If You Love for Beauty"

If you love for beauty, oh do not love me!
Love the sun, she has golden hair!

If you love for youth, oh do not love me!
Love the spring; it is young every year!

If you love for treasure, oh do not love me!
Love the mermaid; she has many clear pearls!

If you love for love, oh yes, do love me!
Love me ever, I'll love you evermore!

TRANSLATION BY DAVID KENNETH SMITH

Robert Schumann (1810–1856)
"Ich grolle nicht," from *Dichterliebe*

TEXT AND TRANSLATION

"Ich grolle nicht," from *Dichterliebe*

Ich grolle nicht, und wenn das Herz auch bricht,
Ewig verlor'nes Lieb! Ich grolle nicht.
Wie du auch strahlst in Diamantenpracht,
Es fällt kein Strahl in deines Herzens Nacht.
Das weiss ich längst.

Ich grolle nicht, und wenn das Herz auch bricht.
Ich sah dich ja im Traume,
Und sah die Nacht in deines Herzens Raume,
Und sah die Schlang', die dir am Herzen frisst,
Ich sah, mein Lieb, wie sehr du elend bist.
Ich grolle nicht.

HEINRICH HEINE

"I Bear No Grudge," from *The Poet's Love*

I bear no grudge, even if my heart is breaking!
Love lost forever! I bear no grudge.
Although you shine in diamond splendor,
no beam falls into the night of your heart.
I have known that for a long time.

I bear no grudge, even if my heart is breaking!
I truly saw you in my dreams
and saw the night in the room of your heart,
and saw the snake that bites your heart;
I saw, my dear, how truly miserable you are.
I bear no grudge.

TRANSLATION BY PAUL HINDEMITH (ADAPTED)

Robert Schumann

"Im wunderschönen Monat Mai," from *Dichterliebe*

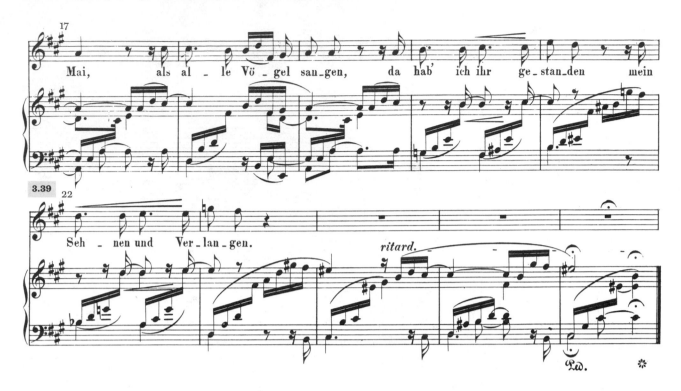

TEXT AND TRANSLATION

"Im wunderschönen Monat Mai," from *Dicterliebe*

"In the Lovely Month of May," from *The Poet's Love*

Im wunderschönen Monat Mai,
Als alle Knospen sprangen,
Da ist in meinem Herzen
Die Liebe aufgegangen.

In the lovely month of May,
when all the buds were bursting,
then within my heart
love broke forth.

Im wunderschönen Monat Mai,
Als alle Vögel sangen,
Da hab' ich ihr gestanden
Mein Sehnen und Verlangen.

In the lovely month of May,
when all the birds were singing,
then I confessed to her
my longing and desire.

HEINRICH HEINE

TRANSLATION BY PHILIP L. MILLER

Robert Schumann
"Trällerliedchen" ("Humming Song"),
from *Album for the Young,* Op. 68, No. 3

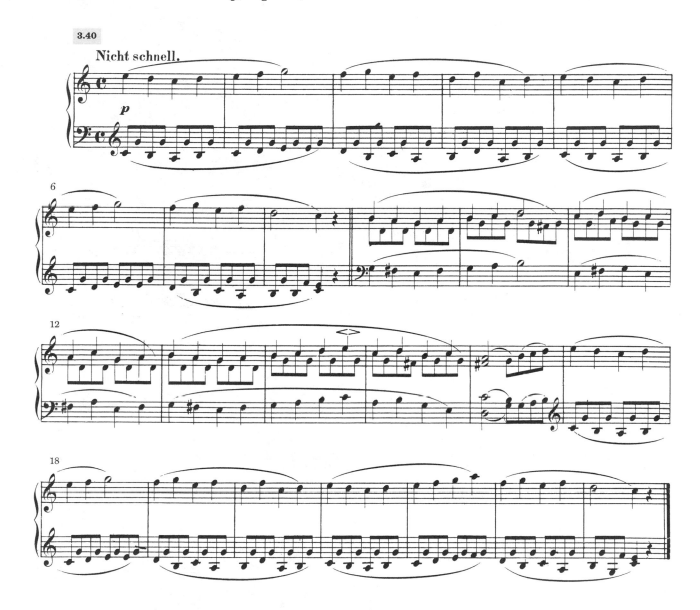

John Philip Sousa (1854–1932)

"The Stars and Stripes Forever"

Piano score

Short score (excerpt)

John Philip Sousa "The Stars and Stripes Forever," short score (excerpt)

John Philip Sousa "The Stars and Stripes Forever," short score (excerpt)

Igor Stravinsky (1882–1971)

"Bransle Gay," from *Agon*

Igor Stravinsky

"Lento," from *For the Five Fingers*

John Tavener (b. 1944)
"The Lamb"

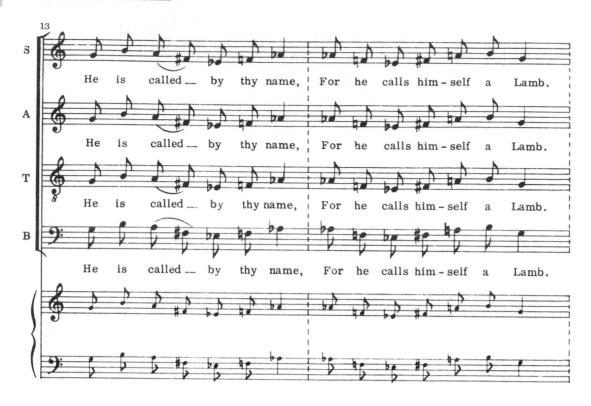

He is called — by thy name, For he calls him-self a Lamb.

He is meek, and he is mild, He be-came a lit – tle child.

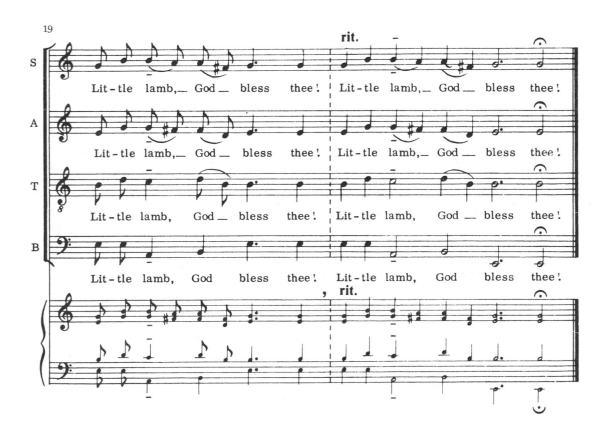

Edgard Varèse (1883–1965)

Density 21.5, for solo flute

Written in January 1936 at the request of Georges Barrère for the inauguration of his platinum flute.
Revised April 1946. 21.5 is the density of platinum.

** Always strictly in time—follow metronomic indications.

*** Notes marked + to be played softly, hitting the keys at the same time to produce a percussive effect.

Anton Webern (1883–1945)

"Dies ist ein Lied," from *Fünf Lieder aus "Der siebente Ring,"* Op. 3, No. 1

TEXT AND TRANSLATION

"Dies ist ein Lied," from *Fünf Lieder aus "Der siebente Ring"*

Dies ist ein Lied
für dich allein;
von kindischem Wähnen,
von frommen Tränen . . .
Durch Morgengärten klingt es
ein leichtbeschwingtes.
Nur dir allein
möcht es ein Lied
das rühre sein.

STEFAN GEORGE

"This Is a Song," from *Five Songs from "The Seventh Ring"*

This is a song
for you alone:
of childish beliefs,
of pious tears . . .
through morning gardens it floats
on light wings.
Only for you
would it like to be a song
that moves the soul.

TRANSLATION BY EMILY EZUST

Anton Webern
String Quartet, Op. 5, third and fourth movements

Anton Webern
Variations for Piano, Op. 27, second movement

Meredith Willson (1902–1984)

"Till There Was You," from *The Music Man*

sky,   but I nev - er saw them wing - ing.   No, I

nev - er saw them at   all,   till there was   you.____

____ And there was mu - sic,   and   there were won - der - ful

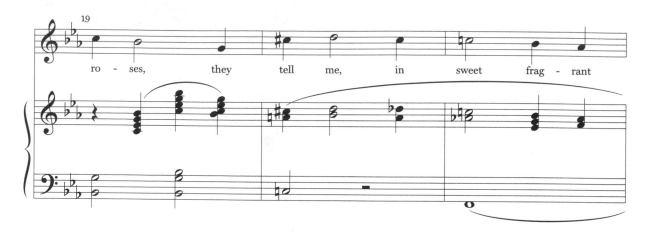

ro - ses,   they   tell   me,   in   sweet   frag - rant

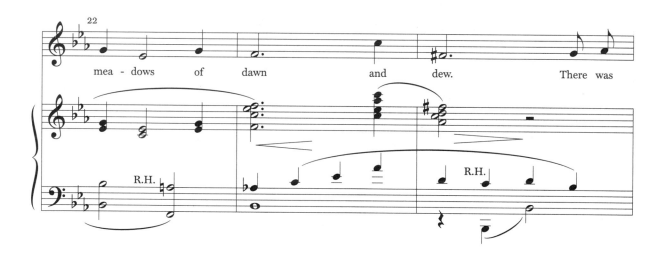

mea - dows   of   dawn   and   dew.   There was

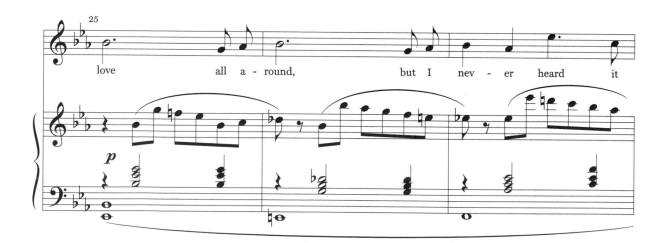

love   all a - round,   but I   nev - er   heard   it

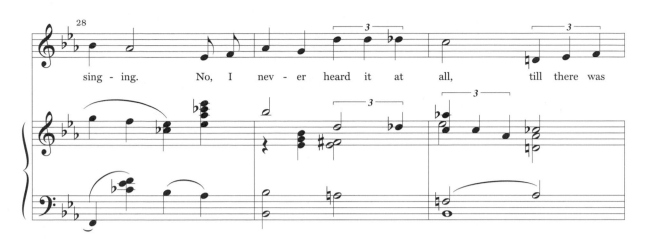

sing - ing.   No, I   nev - er   heard it   at   all,   till there was

you.

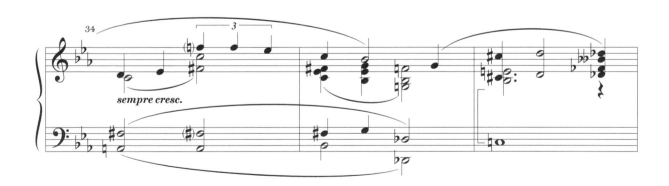

sempre cresc.

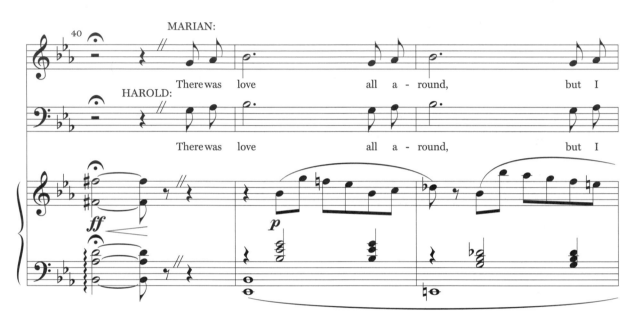

all,   till   there   was   you.

all,   till   there   was   you.

CD Tracks and Performers

Page numbers refer to the Anthology.

CD ONE

1. Anonymous, Minuet in D minor (from the *Anna Magdalena Bach Notebook*) [p. 1]
William Porter, harpsichord
  Track 1: measure 1
  Track 2: measure 9 (second section)

3. Bach, *Brandenburg Concerto* No. 4, second movement [p. 2]
Cologne Chamber Orchestra, Helmut Müller-Brühl, conductor (Naxos 8.554608)
  Track 3: measure 1
  Track 4: measure 65b (final cadence)

Bach, Chorales
Third Presbyterian Church Choir (Rochester, NY); Peter DuBois, conductor

5. "Aus meines Herzens Grunde" (Chorale No. 1) [p. 6]
  Track 5: measure 1
  Track 6: measure 7b

7. "O Haupt voll Blut und Wunden" (Chorale No. 74) [p. 7]
  Track 7: measure 1
  Track 8: measure 2b

9. "Wachet auf" (Chorale No. 179) [p. 8]
  Track 9: measure 1
  Track 10: measure 6b
  Track 11: measure 17b
  Track 12: measure 25b
  Track 13: measure 32b

14. Bach, Invention in D minor [p. 11]
William Porter, harpsichord
  Track 14: measure 1
  Track 15: measure 7
  Track 16: measure 18

17. Bach, Prelude in C Major (from *The Well-Tempered Clavier*, Book I) [p. 13]
William Porter, harpsichord
  Track 17: measure 1
  Track 18: measure 5
  Track 19: measure 7
  Track 20: measure 11

  Track 21: measure 18
  Track 22: measure 24

23. Bach, Chaconne, from Violin Partita No. 2 in D minor [p. 15]
Oleh Krysa, violin
  Track 23: measure 1
  Track 24: measure 25
  Track 25: measure 41

26. Bartók, *Bagatelle*, Op. 6, No. 2 [p. 21]
Robert Wason, piano
  Track 26: measure 1
  Track 27: measure 3
  Track 28: measure 7
  Track 29: measure 10
  Track 30: measure 14
  Track 31: measure 19
  Track 32: measure 24

33. Bartók, "Bulgarian Rhythm," from *Mikrokosmos* (No. 115) [p. 23]
Robert Wason, piano
  Track 33: measure 1
  Track 34: measure 9
  Track 35: measure 17
  Track 36: measure 25

37. Bartók, "Song of the Harvest," for two violins [p. 25]
Timothy Ying and Janet Ying, violins
  Track 37: measure 1
  Track 38: measure 6
  Track 39: measure 11
  Track 40: measure 30

41. Beethoven, Piano Sonata in C minor, Op. 13 (*Pathétique*)
Second movement, Adagio cantabile—Kristian Bezuidenhout, fortepiano [p. 26]
  Track 41: measure 1
  Track 42: measure 5
  Track 43: measure 16b
  Track 44: measure 36b
  Track 45: measure 47
Third movement, Rondo (Allegro)—Sergio Monteiro, piano [p. 30]
  Track 46: measure 1
  Track 47: measure 25
  Track 48: measure 41
  Track 49: measure 78b
  Track 50: measure 120b

51. Beethoven, Piano Sonata in C Major, Op. 53 (*Waldstein*), first movement (Allegro con brio) [p. 37]
Sergio Monteiro, piano
  Track 51: measure 1 (first theme group)
  Track 52: measure 18
  Track 53: measure 35 (second theme group)
  Track 54: measure 43 (second theme varied)
  Track 55: measure 74
  Track 56: measure 112
  Track 57: measure 156 (recapitulation)
  Track 58: measure 167
  Track 59: measure 295

60. Beethoven, Sonatina in F Major, Op. Posth., second movement (Rondo—Allegro) [p. 52]
Sergio Monteiro, piano
  Track 60: measure 1
  Track 61: measure 49
  Track 62: measure 87

63. Brahms, "Die Mainacht" [p. 54]
Elizabeth W. Marvin, soprano; Jean Barr, piano
  Track 63: measure 1
  Track 64: measure 9
  Track 65: measure 33

66. Chance, Variations on a Korean Folk Song (mm. 1–52, 199–end) [p. 59]
Tokyo Kosei Wind Orchestra (Frederick Fennell, conductor)
  Track 66: measure 1
  Track 67: measure 38 (Vivace)
  Track 68: measure 199 ("Con Islancio")

69. Clarke, *Trumpet Voluntary* (*Prince of Denmark's March*) [p. 69]
Douglas Prosser, trumpet; Peter DuBois, organ
  Track 69: measure 1
  Track 70: measure 4
  Track 71: measure 9
  Track 72: measure 17
  Track 73: measure 49

74. **Clementi, Sonatina in C Major, Op. 36, No. 1, first movement** (Allegro) [p. 76]
Sergio Monteiro, piano
 Track 74: measure 1
 Track 75: measure 5
 Track 76: measure 16
  (second section)
 Track 77: measure 24

78. **Corelli, Allemanda, from Trio Sonata in A minor, Op. 4, No. 5** [p. 78]
Timothy Ying, Janet Ying, and David Ying, strings, with William Porter, harpsichord
 Track 78: measure 1
 Track 79: measure 9
 Track 80: measure 13
  (second section)
 Track 81: measure 22b

82. **Corigliano, "Come now, my darling," from *The Ghosts of Versailles*** [p. 81]
Elizabeth W. Marvin, soprano; Kathryn Cowdrick, mezzo-soprano; Jean Barr, piano
 Track 82: measure 1 (recitative)
 Track 83: measure 10
 Track 84: measure 38 (aria/duet)

85. **Dallapiccola, "Die Sonne kommt," from *Goethe-lieder*, for voice and clarinets** [p. 87]
Heather Gardner, soprano; Juliet Grabowski, clarinet
 Track 85: measure 1
 Track 86: measure 6

87. **Gershwin, "I Got Rhythm"** [p. 88]
Elizabeth W. Marvin, soprano; Robert Wason, piano
 Track 87: measure 1
 Track 88: measure 3
 Track 89: measure 37
 Track 90: measure 45

91. **Gershwin, " 'S Wonderful!"** [p. 94]
Robert Swensen, tenor; Kathryn Cowdrick, mezzo-soprano; Robert Wason, piano
 Track 91: measure 1
 Track 92: measure 5 (verse)
 Track 93: measure 29 (refrain)

94. **"Greensleeves"** [p. 99]
Petar Kodzas, guitar
 Track 94: measure 1
 Track 95: measure 29

CD TWO

1. **Handel, Chaconne in G Major, from *Trois Leçons*** [p. 100]
William Porter, harpsichord
 Track 1: measure 1
 Track 2: measure 49 (var. 6)
 Track 3: measure 57 (var. 7)
 Track 4: measure 73 (var. 9)
 Track 5: measure 89 (var. 11)

 Track 6: measure 97 (var. 12)
 Track 7: measure 105 (var. 13)
 Track 8: measure 121 (var. 15)
 Track 9: measure 129 (var. 16)

10. **Handel, "Rejoice greatly," from *Messiah*** [p. 107]
Elizabeth W. Marvin, soprano; Peter DuBois, organ
 Track 10: measure 1
 Track 11: measure 7
 Track 12: measure 11
 Track 13: measure 18
 Track 14: measure 20
 Track 15: measure 24
 Track 16: measure 49

17. **Haydn, Piano Sonata No. 9 in F Major, third movement** (Scherzo) [p. 117]
Kristian Bezuidenhout, fortepiano
 Track 17: measure 1
 Track 18: measure 16b

19. **Hensel, "Nachtwanderer"** [p. 118]
Kathryn Cowdrick, mezzo-soprano; Russell Miller, piano
 Track 19: measure 1
 Track 20: measure 14
 Track 21: measure 34

22. **Hensel, "Neue Liebe, neues Leben"** [p. 122]
Robert Swensen, tenor; Russell Miller, piano
 Track 22: measure 1
 Track 23: measure 26b
 Track 24: measure 56b
 Track 25: measure 66b
 Track 26: measure 69
 Track 27: measure 75

28. **Joplin, "Pine Apple Rag"** [p. 127]
Tony Caramia, piano
 Track 28: measure 1
 Track 29: measure 5
 Track 30: measure 53
 Track 31: measure 69
 Track 32: measure 77

33. **Joplin, "Solace"** [p. 131]
Tony Caramia, piano
 Track 33: measure 1
 Track 34: measure 5
 Track 35: measure 17
 Track 36: measure 53
 Track 37: measure 72
 Track 38: measure 80

39. **Joplin, "Solace" bonus track; performance practice** (live performance)
Tony Caramia, piano

40. **Mozart, Piano Sonata in G Major, K. 283, first movement** (Allegro) [p. 135]
Kristian Bezuidenhout, fortepiano
 Track 40: measure 1
  (first theme group)
 Track 41: measure 16b
 Track 42: measure 23

  (second theme group)
 Track 43: measure 31
 Track 44: measure 45
 Track 45: measure 51
 Track 46: measure 54
  (development)
 Track 47: measure 71b
  (recapitulation)

48. **Mozart, Piano Sonata in D Major, K. 284, third movement** [p. 139]
Kristian Bezuidenhout, fortepiano
Theme
 Track 48: measure 1
 Track 49: measure 4b
 Track 50: measure 8b
 Track 51: measure 13b
Var. VII
 Track 52: measure 1
 Track 53: measure 3
 Track 54: measure 5
 Track 55: measure 8b
Var. XII
 Track 56: measure 25b

57. **Mozart, Piano Sonata in C Major, K. 545**
Kristian Bezuidenhout, fortepiano
First movement, Allegro [p. 149]
 Track 57: measure 1
  (first theme group)
 Track 58: measure 5
 Track 59: measure 8
 Track 60: measure 11
 Track 61: measure 13
  (second theme group)
 Track 62: measure 18
 Track 63: measure 26
  (closing theme)
 Track 64: measure 29
  (development)
 Track 65: measure 42
  (recapitulation)
 Track 66: measure 58
 Track 67: measure 67
 Track 68: measure 70
Second movement, Andante [p. 152]
 Track 69: measure 1
 Track 70: measure 61
Third movement, Rondo (Allegretto) [p. 155]
 Track 71: measure 1
 Track 72: measure 8b
 Track 73: measure 14b

74. **Mozart, String Quartet in D minor, K. 421, third movement** (Menuetto) [p. 157]
Ying Quartet
 Track 74: measure 1 (Menuetto)
 Track 75: measure 1
  (repeat of first section)
 Track 76: measure 10b
  (second section)
 Track 77: measure 22
 Track 78: measure 29b
 Track 79: measure 39b (Trio)
 Track 80: measure 47b
  (second section of Trio)
 Track 81: measure 55b

Index of Teaching Points

Note: This index may be used in conjunction with the *Index of Music Examples* in the main text to locate teaching points discussed in the text.